D0001937

לזיכרון ולעילוי נשמת

אנדה זימנד בת שמואל

ת.נ.צ.ב.ה.

❧❧

להבדיל בין חיים לחיים, לברכה, הצלחה ואריכות ימים

לילדי

סיריל, עינן, רנה ונסרין

הנרי זימנד

❧❧

In loving memory and elevation of the soul of

Anda Zimand

ת.נ.צ.ב.ה.

❧❧

For blessing, success and long life
To my children

Syril, Ynnan, Rene and Nessrin

Herni Zimand

❧❧

For further information:

The Kabbalah Centre
155 E. 48th St., New York, NY 10017
1062 S. Robertson Blvd., Los Angeles, CA 90035

1.800.Kabbalah
www.kabbalah.com

First Edition, May 2003
Second Edition, May 2004. Printed in Canada

ISBN 1-57189-233-8

KABBALAH

THE 72 NAMES OF GOD

Technology for the Soul™

MEDITATION BOOK

BY YEHUDA BERG

KABBALAH PUBLISHING

www.kabbalah.com™

TABLE OF CONTENTS

INTRODUCTION

Kabbalistic meditation techniques are more than just exercises. They employ a force called *kavanah,* without which there can be no meditation at any effective level. Like all Hebrew words, *kavanah* is tough to translate, emerging in various connotations as concentration, attention, intention, fervor, and devotion. But most of all, it stands for direction. Without the direction of *kavanah,* prayer and meditation are likely, at best, to take practitioners nowhere in particular, or at worst, to a location they really have no need or desire to reach.

Kavanah is the driving force needed to keep a meditation on track. *Kavanah* is the primary force and the letters of the 72 Names are vehicles for drawing in the appropriate spiritual energy. *Kavanah* is the soul of the meditation.

This guide has been prepared to help you discover your *kavanah,* to identify the areas in your life where you need to apply the Names. *Kavanah* is a powerful tool of Kabbalah that is easy to use once you understand it. Set quiet time aside for yourself, as often as you can, to read and reread the meditations. You might find it useful to write them out, over and over, and commit them to memory. Find the way that works best for you.

Another thing to "keep in mind" while using this book is the concept of Certainty. These tools have been given to you by the Creator and they work. It is natural to experience doubt (don't be surprised, it is bound to creep in). The trick is to acknowledge it and say to yourself, "OK, I'm willing to take the risk of looking silly, and I will allow myself to have absolute certainty that these meditations are going to help me improve my life."

One more thing you need to know – the manifestation of the Light you've gained through meditation depends on what you do in the everyday world.

Just as the Israelites had to walk into the waters in order for the miracle to be completed, you must take action to cross whatever Red Seas exist in your life. Meditating on these Names offers you access to great power—it's up to you to plug into it through effort.

Much more could be said about meditation and its importance to Kabbalah and the world. The purpose of this book, however, is not to explain meditation, but to provide you with a resource for doing it. As of this moment, you have all the knowledge you need for meditating on the 72 Names. May they bring you all the joy and fulfillment that you desire, and that the Creator desires for you.

A Note of Thanks to Sarah Switzer:
I deeply appreciate all of your hard work because without your help, this book would not have been possible.

Yehuda Berg

ויהיו

1. TIME TRAVEL

MEDITATION

I look back at the actions in my own life, and honestly accept my mistakes.

My present is the result of those causes, situations and deeds that I created and can correct. I feel the need to change.

I feel [enter your specific correction here, e.g., pain],

and take responsibility for what I have done.

As I concentrate on the moment [enter negativity that you have created],

I steadily, and with conviction, reverse that action

and change my original direction.

Instead of an unkind word, or a squandered opportunity to share Light,

I will speak with kindness.

I will spread joy. The negative seed is uprooted,

and I feel the beginnings of transformation—in myself, in my past and in my future.

2. RECAPTURING THE SPARKS

MEDITATION

I am going to stop the darkness—remove all destructive forces.

I tap into the positive forces in the universe, open myself up for transformation.

I will reclaim my sparks of Light.

Breaking judgment, embracing love and spreading Light to others,

I feel the sacred sparks returning to my soul,

filling my vessel.

3. MIRACLE MAKING

MEDITATION

I am changing my nature:

letting go of my negative temptations, selfishness, envy, anger and self-pity.

Goodbye.

My vessel expands as I embrace love and Light,

creating more room for positive energy.

An opening in my soul, more space, as I accept that change is possible.

More Light and love as I feel the shift beginning to take hold.

I have created the space for a miracle.

4. ELIMINATING NEGATIVE
THOUGHTS

MEDITATION

I feel doubt, uncertainty. I am worried.

I am worried about [enter your concern here].

But I know it is an illusion. These thoughts that bring me down are not real,

and as I face them, they grow smaller and smaller.

They disappear....

I can eliminate all of my dark thoughts.

I reach for the dial of the negative airwaves, the control over my ego,

and turn it down...down...off.

Silence.

My heart is open, and filling with the Light of the Creator—powerful, calming, whole.

I feel warmth and acceptance—of all people, of myself.

I see and hear the sounds of my soul, true signals from the Light.

I feel total certainty.

5. HEALING

MEDITATION

I am not a victim.

The path I take is up to me.

I will be proactive and take control of my current situation.

I am responsible for my own healing, and I can make it happen.

I am suffering from [enter your specific affliction here], but I am healing.

With each breath, I am filled with the Light and restorative power of the Creator.

I focus the Light like a radar beam on the affected area. I see my internal chaos

and push it away with positive energy.

As healing Light fills me, I focus on [enter someone's name who could benefit from healing energy],

sending him/her all the healing Light of the universe and the Creator, filling him/her with love and protection.

6. DREAM STATE

MEDITATION

I am at peace.

As I fall asleep, I clear my mind and allow the Light into my dreams.

My soul is open to truth, to love. I feel its ascension.

Letting go of daily chaos, renewal is mine.

I awake in the morning elevated and recharged.

7. DNA OF THE SOUL

MEDITATION

I feel chaos in my life.

My [relationship, business, etc., enter your concern here] feels disjointed, obscured.

I am confused about [enter here].

I see the chaos, the fragmentation, and I see myself in it. But as I connect to

the power of creation, spiritual Light is shed on the problem and the darkness scatters.

My own chaos is dwarfed as I feel the 22 separate forces of the Creator take over

and order is restored.

The confusion dissipates and the path to clarity is revealed.

My DNA is fortified and strengthened.

I feel powerful and whole—structure emerges.

8. DEFUSING NEGATIVE ENERGY AND STRESS

MEDITATION

The negativity and stress around me will evaporate.

I see the energy field around my body and allow Light and good energy to fill it.

My state of being is uplifted, and the space around me turns positive.

I breathe in…

and as I let the air out, stress and negative tension drift away.

Pressure dissolves,

and energy from others and the outside world is transformed in my sphere.

I feel balance and peace.

9. ANGELIC INFLUENCES

MEDITATION

I will transform my character.

As I close my eyes and reach out into the network of angels in the universe,

I see the particles all around me, and I commit to connecting with the good forces.

I will be more tolerant, sharing and compassionate.

I see an abundance of positive angels

and welcome them into my realm, shutting out the negative influences.

I will drop my ego and allow room for the universe and its good angels

to bring Light into my life.

10. LOOKS CAN KILL: PROTECTION FROM THE EVIL EYE

MEDITATION

In the past, I have given the evil eye to others.

I have passed judgment, bringing greater negativity into the world and upon myself.

I am blocking out this tendency.

I will restrict, and instead bring positive energy and Light to my dealings with others.

Jealousy and envy evaporate,

replaced with kindness.

I feel protection against evil glances and the dark wishes of others as

I release that judgment in myself.

I am creating a greater opening for Light.

11. BANISHING THE REMNANTS
OF EVIL

MEDITATION

I can drive all of the negative forces from my environment.

As I concentrate on my space,

Light pushes away the evil residue, and my environment is now

free from any of the negative forces that might have been lurking here.

I feel secure and open,

and the sphere around me feels pure.

12. UNCONDITIONAL LOVE

MEDITATION

As I focus on unconditional love,

for all people around me, the dark forces within are cast out.

In the past, I have felt hatred for certain people.

Now, as I picture those people in my mind, I feel only love.

Light washes over them, and me,

and I recognize the common thread that we share—the spark of the Creator.

My heart opens as I wish them joy and fulfillment, peace and greater understanding.

We are one soul, as greater compassion and humanity awaken within

for those around me;--my family, friends, neighbors.

Those positive feelings fan out toward all humanity

as love washes over everyone, bringing greater peace, understanding and harmony throughout the world.

13. HEAVEN ON EARTH

MEDITATION

I will experience heaven here on earth—bring the universal messiah to us.

I want to change my state of mind.

As I block out petty misunderstandings and frustrations,

I allow more Light into my soul.

As I concentrate on the changes that I will make internally,

I help spread that Light around, and we move closer to global peace.

The Light of the Creator burns within me,

and I feed it by sharing with others, always, throughout the world.

14. FAREWELL TO ARMS

MEDITATION

I will concentrate on greater tolerance

in order to achieve peace—in my own life, and in the world.

In the past, I have been intolerant about my own [enter your hang-up here].

As I go back to the root of that intolerance, I readjust my thinking.

I embrace what I do not know, and I strive to understand.

I want to wipe out the conflicts I have created in the past,

and replace them with understanding and light.

Instead of focusing on my differences with others, I will look into their soul and see

our shared humanity.

Peaceful solutions will be possible between us, and on a global scale.

15. LONG-RANGE VISION

MEDITATION

I want to get clear about my decision.

As I look into the future, I pull back the curtains of my consciousness,

all ten of them, one by one,

allowing the truth of the situation at hand to present itself.

I drop illusions and false hopes I may have planted in the past,

letting instinct be my guide.

As I remove the veils of illusion, my intuition is strengthened

and I see what's really going on, now and in the future.

I will pay attention to the signs

and follow my path.

ה·ק·ם

16. DUMPING DEPRESSION

MEDITATION

It is time for me to get up and move forward with my life.

I see the setback and feel the pain, and vow,

right now,

to move on.

As I drop my ego, the negative forces that try to block me fall away.

I see greater Light and begin to feel positive energy enter and fill the empty space.

I envision myself moving forward.

I will continue on, with even greater strength and passion than before,

sharing my Light with others and spreading love.

My problems will be resolved by the effort I make to connect with the Light,

and greater joy and fulfillment will be mine as I push ahead.

לאו

17. GREAT ESCAPE

MEDITATION

No more ego.

As I look into my soul, I can feel the sore places where I have been wounded by my ego:

worry over what people think about me, needing to be right, angry when things don't go my way.

As I let it go and reach for Light on a higher plane, those places in my soul open up.

I am free, my shackles are removed as my ego diminishes and I concentrate on what is really important:

love, friends, family, spiritual fulfillment, connection.

It is not all about me and what I need. I will tap into a universal truth.

When I look back at specific past events, I see the role my ego played in the situation,

blocking me from true happiness.

I take that moment and let it go, re-plant the seed so that something positive will grow.

I feel full and strong.

I am free.

18. FERTILITY

MEDITATION

I am consumed by abundance and love.

I have dropped my internal chaos, my ego, and I am concentrating only on creation.

The power of the divine fills my soul and my heart,

and I tap into the upper world and know that I am ready for something huge.

There is space in my consciousness, in my sphere.

I know that I am not the source of abundance,

but the Creator will provide all that I need.

As I concentrate on bringing [a new soul, an idea, etc.] into the physical realm,

I open up my heart and soul to a new life.

19. DIALING GOD

MEDITATION

I will quiet the static that blocks my spiritual path.

I see chaos and difficulties, negative energy that I have created,

standing in the way of my Light source.

One by one, I remove the obstructions.

As I throw them away, the Light becomes brighter and clearer.

I am connected to the Light source.

There is an opening through which my prayers can be answered.

20. VICTORY OVER ADDICTIONS

MEDITATION

I want to stop [enter your addictive behavior here: being reactive, smoking, beating up on myself, etc.].

And I will.

I will liberate my soul from [your addiction here].

I see myself restricting my negative behavior, stopping my addiction and selfish desire.

I let it go as I embrace the Light and drop my old habits.

As more power fills my soul, I watch the selfish impulses lift.

Through the Light, I am transforming.

My soul is opening up, lighter, as I let go of the dependency.

The only addiction I have is for the Light.

21. ERADICATE PLAGUE

MEDITATION

There is no reason for the modern day plagues that affect our world.

As I concentrate on them—AIDS, cancer, nuclear waste, depression—I send out healing

Light, power and love across the world.

A burst of positive energy goes forth from me out into the universe,

cutting down on the negativity in our world.

Light washes over everything,

shutting out the darkness,

stopping new forms of plague before they take hold.

22. STOP FATAL ATTRACTION

MEDITATION

I do not want negative, spiritually bankrupt people in my life.

[Perhaps there is someone in particular you once allowed in and now you want them out. Visualize that person.]

I see them going away.

I am blocking them from my light and energy,

allowing the spirit of the Creator to fill and surround me,

keeping out other negative forces and people.

As more Light flows through me, I attract others full of positive energy.

The destructive forces are pushed away,

and people who carry those traits are blocked out.

23. SHARING THE FLAME

MEDITATION

I tap into the infinite,

the hidden dimension, the ultimate source of strength and Light,

and imagine sharing that joy with all those around me.

Darkness recedes

as I see candles burning across the universe, signifying the spreading of joy and Light.

I ask for the strength and certainty to go out into the world to share goodness

and create greater opportunities for Light, love and compassion.

24. JEALOUSY

MEDITATION

Envious thoughts, hurtful words toward others, jealousy—as I close my eyes,

I open my heart.

I have certainty that the fulfillment I seek is there for me.

All I need to do is make the effort, take the responsibility and connect to the Light.

I am happy for my friends and their good fortune.

I know that the more Light they reveal by their happiness, the more Light there is for me, and for the rest of the world.

I push those old, jealous tendencies out of my soul, allowing Light and compassion to enter.

[If there is a certain person or situation that causes this reaction in you, picture them/it now.]

I am dropping my negative energy toward you and sending only love and Light.

I feel the overwhelming negative forces lifting as I restrict, as I vow to hold back my own dark actions.

More Light is revealed as the upper and lower worlds move back toward alignment,

and I drop my negative tendencies.

25. SPEAK YOUR MIND

MEDITATION

I see a moment in my life, in my past, when I should have spoken my mind.

[Picture yourself in that moment, with the person in question, and imagine what you would have said and how. As you do this, concentrate on opening up, allowing yourself the freedom to speak your mind.]

I will say what needs to be said--to loved ones, friends, those around me—

and free myself from the burden of holding it all in.

I tap into the strength of the Creator for the courage to say what I feel,

which allows me to be closer to others.

At the same time, I am open to what is being said to me—

open to change and understanding,

and able to listen to others.

26. ORDER FROM CHAOS

MEDITATION

Balance and serenity are taking over my life,

pushing out chaos.

I concentrate on seeing the order.

I picture each day of the week, counting slowly to seven, while focusing on each day.

I breathe out as the seven dimensions become aligned,

and Light fills my sphere.

Peace is restored,

making way for positive results.

27. SILENT PARTNER

MEDITATION

I will give back some of what I earn,

allowing more Light and wealth into both my spiritual and physical realms.

As I focus on these three letters, I claim the Light as my silent partner,

removing destructive forces from my financial picture.

I feel freedom from negativity as I strengthen my connection to the Light Force,

knowing that when I ask for sustenance, the Light will provide,

as I will provide positive energy for those around me.

28. SOUL MATE

MEDITATION

I want to find a soul mate,

and bring all of my existing relationships to that level.

I ask the Light to bring me my other half, my spiritual partner.

I want to relate to all those around me on this heightened spiritual plane

and bring greater Light into my life.

My soul mate is out there, and I want to draw him/her closer.

29. REMOVING HATRED

MEDITATION

I am going to be honest and clear

and remove the hatred from my heart.

I feel [enter your problem emotion here: envy, malice, hatred, etc.]

toward [enter person or groups],

and I will let it go.

As Light fills my heart and soul, disgust and intolerance drift away,

replaced by compassion and understanding.

I am filled with love, and the negative forces are dropped from within.

I feel love for all people around me,

and release hatred from my soul.

אוים

30. BUILDING BRIDGES

MEDITATION

Om.

Repeating over and over…Om.

I am connecting to the highest spiritual plane.

In this physical realm, I concentrate on people,

on relationships that need repair or rebuilding.

And I go back to the source, the root of the problem, and let it go.

I reconnect to people with love and Light,

strengthening our bond with compassion and understanding.

I see a Light connection to the upper world,

made stronger as I feed it with positive energy.

I envision myself reaching out to those people—right now!—and, in so doing,

building yet another bridge to a higher spiritual level.

Om.

31. FINISH WHAT YOU START

MEDITATION

[Think of an unfinished project that is an obstacle in your life. Decide you are going to finish it and follow through, and begin this meditation.]

I see the unfinished project in front of me.

I am going to complete [enter project here]

as I visualize myself [enter the process necessary for completion here].

I feel frustration and procrastination drifting away.

I am getting closer to completing my goal.

As I breathe, I get even closer.

I feel stronger, more connected to my Light Force.

Laziness and doubt are gone,

and I see myself fulfilled,

creating more psychic space for even greater accomplishments.

32. MEMORIES

MEDITATION

I want to break the cycle of mistakes.

I am going to stop [enter your recurring mistake here].

I am particularly bothered by [enter negative memory].

As I see the memory, I pour Light onto it and watch it drift away.

I will not let [enter negative memory here] re-enter my consciousness.

I have cleared the way with positive energy, eradicating the bad feelings.

I have the power to fully let go, to live in the moment.

When the same mistake or rut comes my way in the future, it will not affect me—

I have changed course.

33. REVEALING THE DARK SIDE

MEDITATION

Why are bad things happening to me?

Or, why do I feel as if I'm spinning my wheels?

I concentrate on the sequence of letters and ask the Light to illuminate my nature,

to show me where I can make improvements in myself.

Reactive behavior, my ego, all negativity that might taint my soul—

I want it out.

I will push it away and pay attention to the circumstances around me.

I'll spend each day spreading Light and joy in the world,

sharing with those around me.

34. FORGET THYSELF

MEDITATION

I am going to get out of the way and allow the tree of life to lift me up.

In the past, I have been stubborn, set in my ways, and I will let go.

Instead of clinging to my beliefs, I will open up,

allow the Light of the upper dimension to shine down into my realm

and transform my life.

I have real desire,

not for myself alone, but to connect to something greater.

Letting go of my ego and stepping aside,

I feel the divine Force taking over.

35. SEXUAL ENERGY

MEDITATION

I will approach sex with passion, fully present,

putting my lover's needs before my own.

When we are together, we will be a part of the divine universe,

fully connected to the Light and love that we are generating.

During sex I will be tuned in,

letting go of my own desires

and allowing the genuine care and unity I share with my partner

to radiate into the cosmos.

36. FEAR(LESS)

MEDITATION

I will work through my fears and find paradise.

I have been frozen by [enter your fears here],

but I will no longer allow it/them to stop me.

I am breaking through, creating my own Light and positive energy

as I transform my soul.

I take each of my fears and throw them away—

they are gone, banished from my realm.

I will not run away.

I will go forward and through, lifting up and confronting what frightens me.

Happiness and fulfillment are mine.

I will remain connected,

no longer settling or coping,

but spreading Light

and living a divine life.

37. THE BIG PICTURE

MEDITATION

I will see more deeply into my life,

into my consciousness,

and fully understand the seeds I am planting.

I notice the correlation between cause and effect in my own life,

and I understand where I am going.

I will spread love and Light, knowing that they are what await me tomorrow.

I will bring joy and fulfillment to others, knowing that that is what will fill the world around me.

I will focus on the big picture, the plans of the divine Creator,

and connect to that Light source.

38. CIRCUITRY

MEDITATION

I will concentrate on receiving for the purpose of sharing.

Letting go of my desire to receive for myself alone,

I allow Light and prosperity into my realm, connecting me to the divine circuitry of life.

By giving and receiving with the right consciousness, for others,

I will not share only that I may get something back,

and I will not take from others for the wrong reasons.

I will spread Light and share, knowing that blessings await me,

that I will get everything I need from sharing with others.

39. DIAMOND IN THE ROUGH

MEDITATION

I have the power to transform all of my hardships into beauty and strength.

I will get into a positive head space, knowing that from there, anything is possible.

The challenges that lie before me are there for a reason,

and the Light will allow me to learn from them and grow—

I become my potential.

All the blessings that are already mine will bring even more fulfillment and joy.

My soul's longings will be answered

and my "negative" situations will turn beautiful.

40. SPEAKING THE RIGHT WORDS

MEDITATION

I silence my ego and restrict.

I will not defame others, gossip or say hurtful things.

I am quiet as I connect to the Light and allow the divine to be my guide,

to speak through me.

As a channel for the Light, I speak words of Light—love, hope and positive energy.

My words will elevate my soul and the souls of others,

instead of bringing me, and others, down.

41. SELF-ESTEEM

MEDITATION

God is within.

I connect to the divine power in my soul and awaken an incredible source.

My own confidence is fortified so that I am empowered to solve my
own problems,

to eradicate the chaos and confusion in my life.

I am aware of the good within and the good that I can do

if I choose to take responsibility for the Light in me.

It has always been there--

now I see it.

As I concentrate on the sequence of letters, I feel the power of the
high priests,

and it fills me.

42. REVEALING THE CONCEALED

MEDITATION

I tap into the universal truths.

Light from the Creator shines upon me,

and I am able to see what is actually happening.

My powers of observation are strengthened

and I connect to the truth,

to what has been concealed until now.

43. DEFYING GRAVITY

MEDITATION

I am throwing away my doubts, pessimism and limited nature—

I want to see beyond the illusions!

I am listening to my soul and dropping my ego,

making way for real fulfillment.

I possess the powers of mind over matter,

and I will use them by letting go of the limited thinking of the rational mind.

By putting the spiritual above the physical, everything is possible.

44. SWEETENING JUDGMENT

MEDITATION

I will spread love for no reason.

I will resist my tendencies toward judgment.

As I look back on negative words or deeds from my past,

I replace them with Light and compassion,

sending positive forces out into the universe to replace the negative ones at play.

I will look upon others with compassion—

sweetening the judgments—

as they come my way.

45. THE POWER OF PROSPERITY

MEDITATION

I transcend my financial burdens

and allow the Light to provide for me.

As prosperity grows, I continue to share, to give back more to others.

I will not obsess about money.

I distance myself from my money issues,

acknowledging that in my desire for it, perhaps I have lost out on other parts of my life.

And as I open up the channel for actual prosperity, I feel even greater abundance,

an endless supply of Light.

Infinite fulfillment awaits me.

46. ABSOLUTE CERTAINTY

MEDITATION

I have absolute certainty that what is right will happen,

through proactive behavior.

I take complete responsibility for my life and know that

I am getting what I need right now.

And as I continue to allow more Light and certainty into my life, I will get even more.

I see past doubts, and banish them from my realm.

Filled with certainty and trust, there is no room for ambiguities.

My conviction is strong.

Absolute certainty, in all areas of my life, is mine.

47. GLOBAL TRANSFORMATION

MEDITATION

A revolution is possible.

On a personal and global scale, I can change the world--

and I will.

I concentrate on increasing the happiness in my own life

so that I may share it with others.

There are traits of mine that I want to let go

[enter those traits here]

as I transform into a more giving, compassionate person.

As Light spreads within me and I grasp the power of the Creator,

I imagine love spreading to everyone in the universe.

I look into the world and see changes that need to be made,

and know that they are a reflection of what I must do internally.

I concentrate on letting peace into my heart,

and allowing it to radiate throughout the world.

48. UNITY

MEDITATION

I will let go of my desire to be right.

Happiness is more important to me than being right.

I will strive to be less reactive, to accept the beliefs and ways of others,

and to look upon them with compassion and understanding.

As I foster unity in my own relationships and life, I let go of old, tired beliefs,

frustrations that are weighing me down and blocking my soul from total fulfillment.

I will look at all sides of situations with understanding

and an open heart and mind.

49. HAPPINESS

MEDITATION

I am dropping my ego

and moving toward actual and lasting fulfillment.

I will restrain my selfish longings as I ask for what my soul needs,

not what my ego wants.

Looking ahead, I want elevation for my soul, real transformation.

I will restrict my dark impulses and tendencies toward negativity, complaining.

I appreciate everything around me,

and reach into my soul at the deepest level to connect with real happiness and true joy.

50. ENOUGH IS NEVER ENOUGH

MEDITATION

I will not settle for less, in any area of my life.

[If there is a particular area in which you are settling, meditate on that.]

I want everything that is possible.

I want to banish all the darkness and doubts from my life—and I will.

I let go of everything that prevents me from having it all,

including eternal happiness, peace on earth.

All things wonderful are possible,

and I will make them a part of my daily existence.

51. NO GUILT

MEDITATION

[Recall misdeeds from the past, or negative traits of yours that may have harmed another.]

I understand and take responsibility for the pain and suffering that I may have caused,

and as I travel back in time to that moment,

I send compassion and Light to [that person you harmed].

I am looking at the deed, the unkind word, and darkness that I created,

and I am eradicating it from the universe,

replacing it instead with Light, joy and love.

I ask the Creator to repair my dark side and grant me repentance.

I feel the Light wash over and purify me.

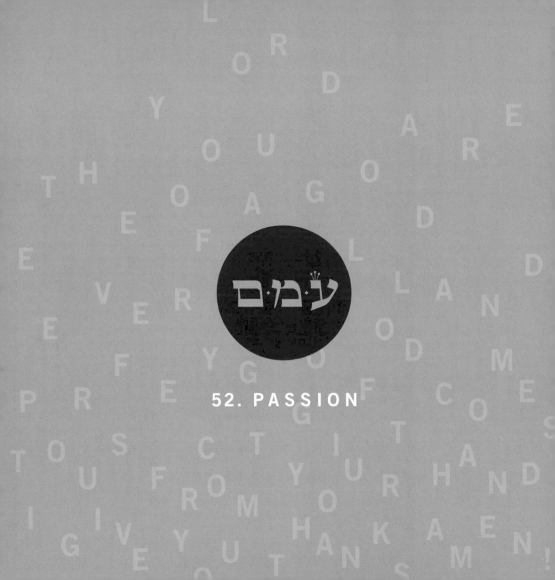

52. PASSION

MEDITATION

As I meditate on the sequence of letters,

I feel the power of passion filling my heart and soul.

Sincerity, devotion and yearning for connection to the Creator

drive my prayers and meditations.

My consciousness opens up

and connects me fully to the upper world.

53. NO AGENDA

MEDITATION

I will drop my agenda and ulterior motives.

As I cut the strings that I have attached to my giving in the past,

I make room for pure sharing,

giving to others just for the sake of connecting to the Light.

Any favors or payback that I have been expecting, I will now drop—

because they create false connections.

I want nothing in return.

I will give unconditional love and Light to those around me

and reap the greater benefits,

tapping into the ultimate source of strength.

54. THE DEATH OF DEATH

MEDITATION

I am afraid that my [insert the area that you want continuity in your life i.e. relationship, health, sustenance, growth] is coming to an end.

As I meditate on the sequence, I drive the angel of death away,

so that good things in my life do not come to an end…

so that good things on this planet do not come to an end.

Greater Light is revealed to all of us as the angel of death is banished once and for all.

55. THOUGHT INTO ACTION

MEDITATION

I am going to follow through on my plans and ideas.

As I concentrate on [enter a goal/project you squandered],

I imagine following through with it.

I stick to my intentions, revealing more Light as I get closer to their actualization.

Certainty is absolute, as the upper and lower worlds come together in unison.

Letting go of procrastination and seizing the moment to move forward with my ideas,

I set my sights on my ultimate goal.

פוּרִי

56. DISPELLING ANGER

MEDITATION

I will purge anger from my heart,

free my soul of the burden that comes with reacting to the external.

[Envision a recent moment when you lost your temper, and understand what false idol you were worshipping.]

As I recall [think of the moment of anger], I see that I was swayed by the darkness.

I gave power to the situation instead of taking a moment to pull back, of restricting,

and keeping the real power in my own hands.

As I invoke this name, I realize that nothing in the physical world

can cause me to react with anger.

I embrace my own happiness and peace of mind,

and remember that they are generated from within.

As I allow those feelings to burst forth, a tendency to rage and anger dissolves.

I will not be swayed by the false idols.

57. LISTENING TO YOUR SOUL

MEDITATION

I want to connect to my personal mission,

see my spiritual goal.

As I get quiet and let my mind clear, I listen to the stirrings of my soul.

I am here for a higher purpose, a larger reason that I will connect to.

Allowing all of the clutter in my realm to dissolve,

I see a clear picture,

and I am guided only by the Light.

Peace and happiness fill me and radiate out into the world.

We move closer to being one unified soul.

58. LETTING GO

MEDITATION

I am letting go.

Of past pain, regret, trauma.

All of it.

Drifting away.

[If there is a particular theme or moment that you keep coming back to, picture it in your mind. As you do this meditation, go back to that moment, then reverse it, plant a new seed.]

I will release past emotions that are dragging me down,

replacing old baggage with Light and love.

I look forward, not back.

I drop it.

All of it.

Let it go.

59. UMBILICAL CORD

MEDITATION

I look back at my negative actions and harsh judgments.

I will not allow my connection to divine inspiration be cut off.

I will share and spread Light with others so that I can maintain

a constant connection to the Creator.

In moments of darkness, I know that the Light is there,

waiting for me to plug into it.

As I restrict acts of intolerance, my connection grows stronger,

and my Light will not be severed.

60. FREEDOM

MEDITATION

I clearly see my personal limitations.

Looking into the past, I notice all of the instances when ego has kept me imprisoned,

holding me back from true joy and fulfillment.

As I focus on the Light of the Creator, the transformative energy of the divine

washes over me, and I feel free.

No more complaining, no more frustration.

I will not get caught up in the material world.

Instead, I will look beyond into the spiritual realm

and let go,

freeing myself from the trappings of ego.

61. WATER

MEDITATION

As I concentrate on the sequence of letters,

I imagine all of the water within my body clarifying.

I am breathing in Light,

and as I do, it cleanses me.

I feel stronger,

purer.

Continuing to breathe in the Light,

I envision all of the bodies of water in the world becoming clear,

returning to their natural, unpolluted state.

Again, I focus internally, and I see my soul clearing—

all of the hatred, negativity, washing away.

Breathing in,

and then out.

I feel healed and rejuvenated.

62. PARENT—TEACHER, NOT PREACHER

MEDITATION

I will share the Light lovingly and respectfully with my child(ren).

I will not tell them what to do.

Instead, I will show them, sharing the Light and radiance of the Creator in a loving way.

I will teach instead of preach,

opening up the spiritual world and revealing even more Light for them.

[Say your children's names]:

I will give you only love and Light and compassion.

I will guide you along the spiritual path with openness, tolerance

and, most of all, love.

עֵרֶךְ

63. APPRECIATION

MEDITATION

I am quiet,

and my soul opens.

As I think about my life, I see all that is good.

All that I sometimes fail to see is because of my own darkness.

I am filled with gratitude.

The Light of the Creator shines upon me,

and I am filled with abundance and joy.

As I take time each day to appreciate all of my blessings, the Light fulfills my desire.

I live fully in each moment.

Instead of looking back with regret, I concentrate on appreciating what I have now,

and what I will continue to have.

64. CASTING YOURSELF IN A
FAVORABLE LIGHT

MEDITATION

I will allow the Light in me to shine,

and concentrate on revealing the positive side of myself, my soul.

As I show that side of myself, my negativity will diminish

and the Light around all of us will be radiant.

I will see the good in others,

and, in doing so, will give them the best version of me.

65. FEAR OF GOD

MEDITATION

God loves me and only desires my well being.

I have nothing to fear.

I can and will undo my past negative actions,

actions that wreaked havoc in my own life.

I realize that for all of my actions, there is a universal reaction,

and that I can plant positive seeds.

I will share love and kindness with others,

drop my nasty behavior and tap into the eternal Light.

66. ACCOUNTABILITY

MEDITATION

I am not a victim.

All of my feelings of self-pity and regret, and my hopes of retaliation
are vanishing

as I accept the consequences of my own actions.

I take responsibility for where I am,

and know that if I want to change my circumstances, it is within my control.

I will be proactive, and achieve my own fulfillment.

I am letting go of pain, and regaining control over my life.

I will not wallow or be held back because of assumed situations—

they are there because of my actions and I will change them.

Now.

67. GREAT EXPECTATIONS

MEDITATION

My doubt and hopelessness is disappearing.

As I look back at my acts of faith and goodwill, I recognize that they were not for nothing.

They were an opportunity for me to spread goodwill and Light,

and all of that spiritual energy will come back to me.

I am exercising my free will, focusing on everything that I have now,

knowing that there is greater fulfillment and Light

as long as I resist my impulses.

Dropping my great expectations of others, I connect fully to the Light.

68. CONTACTING DEPARTED SOULS

MEDITATION

I meditate upon you [enter name of a departed soul here]

and send you Light and healing energy.

I am quiet,

and our souls are connecting as love flows between us.

I listen for your wisdom and guidance,

feeling your support.

And I continue to send love,

elevating your soul,

and my own.

69. LOST AND FOUND

MEDITATION

I want to find my way back home.

I meditate on the sequence of letters, and the path before me
becomes clearer,

more distinct.

I let go of confusion.

I feel confidence,

certainty

and a sense of direction.

70. RECOGNIZING DESIGN
BENEATH DISORDER

MEDITATION

There is a greater sense of purpose in the world.

There is a perfect system, a flawless order.

I reach for the Light and connect to that higher level.

Doubt and panic that now feel overwhelming are drifting away as I breathe in,

concentrating on the Light.

I embrace structure and serenity, allowing them to take hold in my sphere.

Random occurrences no longer seem so,

as the ultimate design emerges.

71. PROPHECY AND PARALLEL
UNIVERSES

MEDITATION

I will drop my ego and seize the positive reality.

I will restrict negative actions

and choose the right movie for myself.

I will be proactive, determining my fate at each turn,

and continuing to follow the path of the Light.

The power of prophecy is mine,

and with heightened consciousness, I will continually enter new and fulfilling universes.

מים

72. SPIRITUAL CLEANSING

MEDITATION

No more cynicism.

I will not be jaded, nor give others attitude.

I will transform my life.

Dropping my ego, I will take the path of proactive transformation.

If sickness, heartache, financial woes or other problems arise,

I will work through them to connect to the Light,

making the job of transformation my own.

I concentrate on the sequence, purifying iniquities from previous lives.

My spiritual slate is clean

as I allow the Light to engulf my physical and spiritual realms.

72 NAMES CHART

כהת	אכא	ללה	מהֵש	עלם	סיט	ילי	והו
הקֶם	הרי	מבה	יזל	ההֵע	לאו	אלד	הזי
וזהו	מלה	ייי	נלך	פהל	לוו	כלי	לאו
ושֵׁר	לכב	אום	ריי	שׁאה	ירת	האא	נתה
ייז	רהֵע	ועֵם	אני	מנֵד	כוק	להו	יוהו
מייה	עֵשׁל	ערי	סאל	ילה	וול	מיכ	ההה
פֵוי	מבה	נית	ננא	עמם	הוֹשׁ	דני	והו
מוזי	ענו	יהה	ומֵב	מצֵר	הרֵו	ייל	נמם
מום	היי	יבֵם	ראה	וזבו	איע	מנֵק	דֵמֵב

LIST OF 72 NAMES (TRANSLITERATIONS)

01	והו	VAV HEY VAV	(Time Travel)
02	ילי	YUD LAMED YUD	(Recapturing the Sparks)
03	סיט	SAMECH YUD TET	(Miracle Making)
04	עלם	AYIN LAMED MEM	(Eliminating Negative Thoughts)
05	מהש	MEM HEY SHIN	(Healing)
06	ללה	LAMED LAMED HEY	(Dream State)
07	אכא	ALEPH KAF ALEPH	(DNA of the Soul)
08	כהת	KAF HEY TAV	(Defusing Negative Energy and Stress)
09	הזי	HEY ZAYIN YUD	(Angelic Influences)
10	אלד	ALEPH LAMED DALED	(Looks Can Kill)
11	לאו	LAMED ALEPH VAV	(Banishing the Remnants of Evil)
12	ההע	HEY HEY AYIN	(Unconditional Love)
13	יזל	YUD ZAYIN LAMED	(Heaven on Earth)
14	מבה	MEM BET HEY	(Farewell to Arms)
15	הרי	HEY RESH YUD	(Long Range Vision)
16	הקם	HEY KUF MEM	(Dumping Depression)
17	לאו	LAMED ALEPH VAV	(Great Escape)
18	כלי	KAF LAMED YUD	(Fertility)
19	לוו	LAMED VAV VAV	(Dialing God)
20	פהל	PEY HEY LAMED	(Victory Over Addictions)
21	נלך	NUN LAMED KAF	(Eradicate Plague)
22	ייי	YUD YUD YUD	(Stop Fatal Attraction)
23	מלה	MEM LAMED HEY	(Sharing the Flame)
24	וזהו	CHET HEY VAV	(Jealousy)
25	נתה	NUN TAV HEY	(Speak Your Mind)

26	הֲאא	HEY ALEPH ALEPH	(Order from Chaos)
27	ירת	YUD RESH TAV	(Silent Partner)
28	שׂאה	SHIN ALEPH HEY	(Soul Mate)
29	ריי	RESH YUD YUD	(Removing Hatred)
30	אום	ALEPH VAV MEM	(Building Bridges)
31	לכב	LAMED KAF BET	(Finish What You Start)
32	וּשׂר	VAV SHIN RESH	(Memories)
33	יוזו	YUD CHET VAV	(Revealing the Dark Side)
34	לֹהוו	LAMED HEY CHET	(Forget Thyself)
35	כוּק	KAF VAV KUF	(Sexual Energy)
36	מֹנד	MEM NUN DALED	(Fear(less))
37	אנֹי	ALEPH NUN YUD	(The Big Picture)
38	ווֹעם	CHET AYIN MEM	(Circuitry)
39	רהֹע	RESH HEY AYIN	(Diamond in the Rough)
40	יין	YUD YUD ZAYIN	(Speaking the Right Words)
41	ההה	HEY HEY HEY	(Self-Esteem)
42	מֹיכ	MEM YUD KAF	(Revealing the Concealed)
43	ווֹל	VAV VAV LAMED	(Defying Gravity)
44	ילֹה	YUD LAMED HEY	(Sweetening Judgement)
45	סאל	SAMECH ALEPH LAMED	(The Power of Prosperity)
46	עֹרי	AYIN RESH YUD	(Absolute Certainty)
47	עֹשׂל	AYIN SHIN LAMED	(Global Transformation)
48	מֹיה	MEM YUD HEY	(Unity)
49	והֹו	VAV HEY VAV	(Happiness)
50	דֹני	DALED NUN YUD	(Enough Is Never Enough)

51	הוֹשֵׁ	HEY CHET SHIN	(No Guilt)
52	עֳמֵם	AYIN MEM MEM	(Passion)
53	נֳנֳא	NUN NUN ALEPH	(No Agenda)
54	נֳית	NUN YUD TAV	(The Death of Death)
55	מֵבֵה	MEM BET HEY	(Thought into Action)
56	פֶוְי	PEY VAV YUD	(Dispelling Anger)
57	נֳמֵם	NUN MEM MEM	(Listening to Your Soul)
58	יְיֵל	YUD YUD LAMED	(Letting Go)
59	הרְוֹ	HEY RESH CHET	(Umbilical Cord)
60	מֵצֵר	MEM ZADIK RESH	(Freedom)
61	וֵמֵב	VAV MEM BET	(Water)
62	יֵהֵה	YUD HEY HEY	(Parent—Teacher, Not Preacher)
63	עֳנֵו	AYIN NUN VAV	(Appreciation)
64	מֵוְוֹי	MEM CHET YUD	(Casting Yourself in a Favorable Light)
65	דֵמֵב	DALED MEM BET	(Fear of God)
66	מֳנֳק	MEM NUN KUF	(Accountability)
67	אֵיֵע	ALEPH YUD AYIN	(Great Expectations)
68	וֹזֵבֵו	CHET BET VAV	(Contacting Departed Souls)
69	רֵאֵה	RESH ALEPH HEY	(Lost and Found)
70	יֵבֵמֵ	YUD BET MEM	(Recognizing Design Beneath Disorder)
71	הֵיֵי	HEY YUD YUD	(Prophecy and Parallel Universes)
72	מֵוֵם	MEM VAV MEM	(Spiritual Cleansing)